Borrowed Feathers

AND OTHER FABLES

Borrowed Feathers

AND OTHER FABLES

Illustrated by Freire Wright and Michael Foreman

Edited by Bryna Stevens

031663

RANDOM HOUSE 🏠 NEW YORK

Copyright © 1977 by Michael Foreman and Freire Wright. All rights reserved under International and Pan-American Copyright Conventions. Published in the United States by Random House, Inc., New York, and simultaneously in Canada by Random House of Canada Limited, Toronto. Library of Congress Catalog Card Number: 77-79844. ISBN: 0-394-83622-7. Manufactured in the United States of America.   TRADE   ISBN: 0-394-83730-4.   1 2 3 4 5 6 7 8 9 0

BORROWED FEATHERS

A crow flew over a garden wall
and spied some lovely peacock feathers.

"Won't I look handsome in these!"
he said as he proudly tucked the
colorful feathers in among his own.

Then back he flew to his friends, the common birds. "I'm really much too grand a bird for the likes of you," he said, strutting back and forth. "I shall go make friends with the peacocks."

But the peacocks were very angry. "How dare you copy us!" they said. They grabbed at the borrowed feathers, and even pulled out some of the crow's as well.

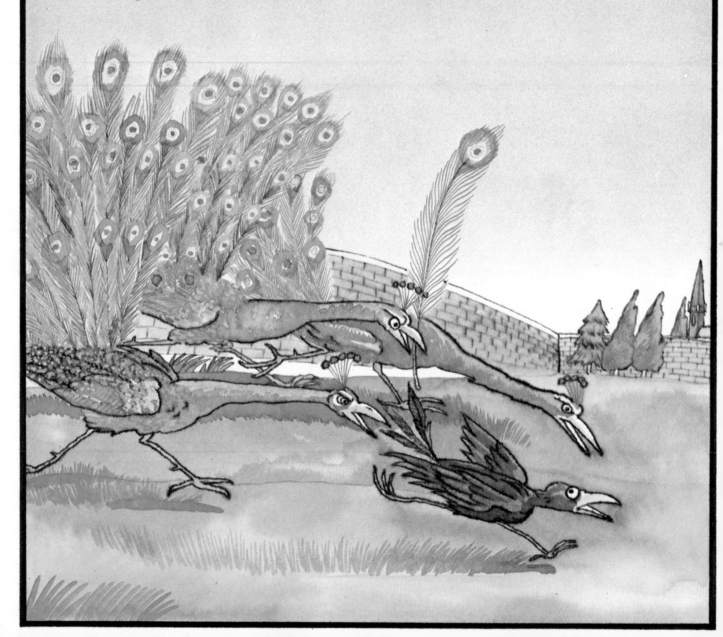

Poor crow! He flew back to his
old friends, the common birds,
as fast as he could go.

But the common birds had not forgotten how shamefully the crow had treated them. They refused to have anything more to do with him.

Borrowed feathers don't make happy birds.

THE FOX AND THE GOAT

A fox was walking near a well when he slipped on some wet stones and fell into the water. "Oh, dear!" he cried. "I shall be stuck down here forever." But as luck would have it, a goat passed by.

"Come on in!" the fox shouted. "The water's fine!"

And the silly goat jumped right into the well.

Whereupon the clever fox climbed onto the goat's horns and leaped out of the well to freedom.

"Next time, you silly fool," called the fox,
"don't be in such a hurry to jump!"

Think before you act.

THE NORTH WIND AND THE SUN

The North Wind was
bragging to the gentle Sun. "I am
much stronger than you," he said.

"No, I don't think so," the Sun answered.

"Oh, yes. I can prove it," said the Wind.
"Here comes a traveler. Let us see which one
of us can make him take off his cloak!"

The North Wind was the first to try.
He huffed and puffed, tugging at the cloak
as hard as he could. But the fiercer
the North Wind blew, the tighter
the traveler wrapped his cloak
around himself.

"Now it's my turn," said the Sun.

First he shone gently on the traveler.

And the man loosened his cloak.

Then the Sun smiled warmly on him.

"My," said the man, "that sun feels so good that I don't think I need my cloak at all." And taking it off, he continued on his way.

Kindness works better than force.

THE FOX AND THE CROW

What luck! thought the crow as she flew to a tree with a big piece of cheese she had found. But a hungry fox passed by and saw it. What a nice breakfast *that* would make, he thought.

"How splendid you are!" called the fox to the crow
in a voice as sweet as honey. "Tell me, fair bird!
Is your singing voice as beautiful as your feathers?"

The crow had never before heard such admiring words.
To prove she could sing she opened her beak in a loud *caw!*
Out tumbled the cheese into the fox's mouth.

"In return for my breakfast," said the fox when
he had finished eating, "I will give you some advice...

...Never trust a flatterer!"

THE GREAT AND LITTLE FISHES

"We are the giants of the sea," cried the Great Fishes. "All creatures are afraid of us. But you, Little Fishes, are helpless. You cannot even defend yourselves."

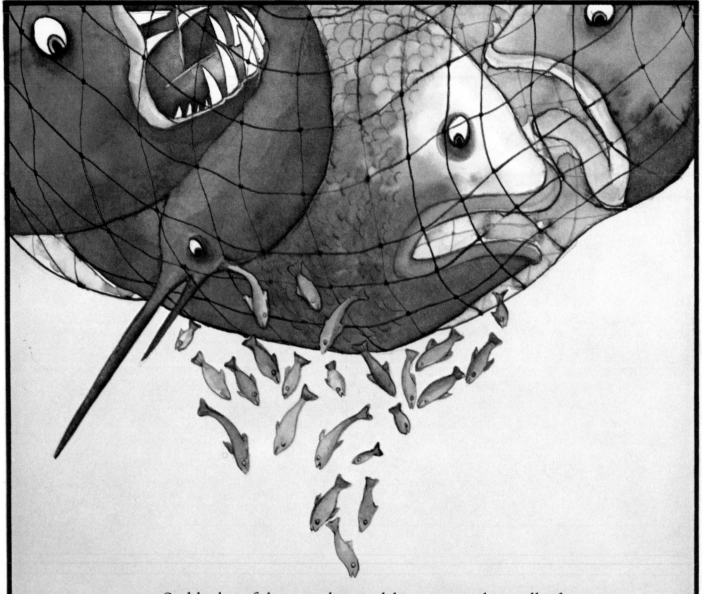

Suddenly a fisherman lowered his net, catching all of
the Great Fishes at one time. But the Little Fishes
easily swam to safety through the holes in the net.

Biggest is not always best.

THE STAG
AND HIS REFLECTION

How beautiful my antlers are, thought the stag, admiring himself in a forest pool. They are like the graceful branches of a tree. But my legs are ugly—nothing but skin and bones.

Just then a hunter's arrow whizzed by.

The stag raced fearfully through the forest.

I must be safe now, thought the stag, running between the trees.

But his antlers suddenly caught in some brambles. The stag was trapped.

Another arrow whizzed through the air, hitting its mark.
The wounded animal moaned. "How foolish I was to admire
my antlers, which have got me caught. My skinny legs,
which I thought were so ugly, almost saved my life."

We often prize that which is least useful.

THE MILKMAID

A country maid was walking to market with a pail of milk on her head. Let's see, she thought. With the money I get when I sell this milk, I shall buy a hen.

Of course, my hen will lay eggs, and they will hatch into cute little chickens. And when my chickens are grown, I shall sell them all. Then I will have enough money to buy myself a new green dress. And maybe some ribbons, too.

How pretty I shall look! All the boys will chase after me, but I will just turn up my nose and walk away.

The country maid gave her head a quick toss.

Down went the pail of milk, spilling every drop.
So all her dreams of eggs, hens, and new dresses
came to nothing.

*Don't count your chickens
before they are hatched.*